Rust & Weeds

Kerry Moyer

Kellogg Press   Topeka, KS

Rust & Weeds
Copyright © 2020 Kerry Moyer

All rights reserved. No part of this publication may be reproduced, distributed, or transmitted in any form or by any means, without prior written permission of the publisher.

This is a work of fiction. The names, characters, places, and incidents are either a product of the author's imagination or used fictitiously, and any resemblance to actual persons living or dead, business establishments, events, or locals is entirely coincidental.

Published by Kellogg Press
Topeka, KS 66606
kelloggpress.com

Printed in the United States of America

Curtis Becker, Project Manager/Copy Editor/Layout & Design/Cover
curtis@curtisbeckerbooks.com

Allysa Hallett, Illustrations

ISBN: 978-0-578-63152-3

Dedicated to Kansas, my people, and everyone who has touched my heart in this life.

Rust & Weeds	1
Muddied	3
That You Might Know Me	4
Adrift	5
The Eastern Dragon and Other Tales of Culinary Intrigue	6
[In Rain]	10
Rising	11
Flint	12
Wrecked	13
Harvest	14
Those Threshing Days	15
Mending	16
Trash Truck	18
Joy	19
Alone	20
Quiet	21

Stare	22
Cocked	23
Pulsing	24
Faces	26
Light	27
Marble	29
Vampire	30
[In Waters]	31
Sun Kil Moon	32
Master	33
The Round	34
Meat Soup	35
Kalashnikov	36
Clicking	37
Like a Breeze	38
Warm Water	39
Brute	40

Iron	41
Dust	42
If I Wrote the Last Poem	44
[In Wind]	45
Cramps	46
Cold Yellow Towel	48
Stained Red	49
Solitude	50
Stubble	51
Weary	53
Unsinkable	55
Age	56
Twenty-Five Years and Not a Stone	57
Missle	58
Night Moves	59
James Wanted to Fight	60
Empty	62

Brick	64
Miles	65
Edward at 13	66
I Ate the Last Cookie	67
Moments	68
Annette Wore Smiles	69
Park Lane	70
Three Rons	71
Four Kittens	72
A Life	74
Orange Shirt	76
Morning Dew	77
The Saddle Boogie Saloon	80
Clanging	82
Sin	83
Mercy	84
Arm's Length	86

December	87
Magnolia	88
Lilacs	90
To Nap	91
Eyes	92
I Wake	94
Fog	95
Damage	96
Worth	97
Sometimes	98
Ghost	99
Sharp Teeth	100
Dusk	101
Sunshine	102
The Patience of Saints	104

In three words I can sum up everything I have learned about life: It goes on.

Robert Frost

Rust & Weeds

Blue water tower
watches over rusted steel bones that
sit on cracked, flat rubber
tires, Fords and Chevys
rot in knee high

grass. A man stands
in his gravel drive
with a gravel look
by a blue Chevy
truck. A brown dog watches
from its wild yard,

vines over the silver
chrome-plated grill
of a rusting, red truck,
and I think it's been years
since that truck did

work. A gray striped tabby slinks
through an old brick schoolhouse,
no roof remaining.
Weeds cover, climb,
pigeons call from
above those red brick

walls. Around a curve,
a white church
flag, hanging, moving
in summer breeze,
and I wonder if anyone
still sits in wooden

Kerry Moyer

pews. A closed post office
by an abandoned auto shop,
buildings boarded up,
cracks and broken glass.
Two faded stop signs
at an intersection,

homes in need of paint
line dirt and gravel streets.
An elderly woman sits,
looks at me, then looks away.
A white Dodge pick-up
rolls

past. There is a park
with a single swing,
a single steel slide.
Rusted goals on rusted poles,
and I think how many years
since children

played. A memorial with mowed
grass, slab swept
for those boys who died
in wars far from here,
names carved
in this place, on polished

stone. This Kansas town,
population aging, fading,
a town at war
with rust and weeds.

Muddied

The rock road,
edged pot holes
deep, with water,
mud edges,
my thoughts deep,
muddied edges,
sun, crouched behind
trees, I've been here
before, rolling on rock,
on a road,
on my bike,
weaving around holes,
dirty water
muddied, my thoughts,
pedaling, pushing
through pedals,
through rock,
through ground,
leaving the day
in my line, stretched out
behind me,
their shadows cast long
in a setting sun
that always finds me,
always sees me
over the edge of trees.

Kerry Moyer

Then You Might Know Me

If you've ever been covered
with blood,
blood from another,
mingled in cuts of your own.

If you've ever punished,
brought down hurt
upon the unlucky bastard
who decided to push and push...

If you've ever stopped to think,
you really can drink enough whiskey
to forget the mess
the mess in your head, your heart...

Then you might know me
Then you might know me...

Adrift

I am soft

 Tortured and taut

  Forged, fraught

   I'm galvanized, weaponized

    I have blood on my hands

    I have love in my heart

    I've had a long road

    I am lost–

      adrift

      a restless sea

        I am haunted
          by thoughts:

            a slave
              to thoughts

                adrift

                  in thought

Kerry Moyer

The Eastern Dragon and Other Tales of Culinary Intrigue

fire leapt
singeing the large nest
of blonde lacquered hair
jutting out from the painted
full face across the table
a nervous laugh squeaks out
as the woman leans back
in her black wooden chair.

Smiling Hibachi Chef
taps, bangs tools
rhythmic ring,
square of butter drops onto
the sizzling silver surface,
onions rings are piled
three high,
oil is poured in and lit,
to my youngest child's delight
and mine.
fire flows like lava
from the flaming stack.

cooked shrimp get tossed
expertly into waiting,
gaping mouths
like circus seals–
and I think
The Hibachi Chef
is the coolest guy in the room!
hell, maybe in the whole damn town.
probably has a sword on the wall
at home with a row of enemy heads

along with his copy of "The Art of War"
open on the nightstand by his bed.

my wife is smiling too much
and I just caught a shrimp–
it took two tries
but I won the briny prize–
pasty white waiter comes out,
refills my tea and asks if we need anything,
his voice is flat, no feeling
never even looks at the Samurai Cook
scraping the blackened surface,
sweat dripping
from His forehead
and still smiling face.

the fire lady
across the way
is primping,
a smile forming
as a small dish
of orange sherbet
is placed in front
of her beaming face–
and I think in spite of the blaze
her hair somehow got larger.

as the Hibachi Chef finishes the show
we clap and I say thank You
meaning every word –
so very little impresses me anymore,
The Chef gives a slight wave,
smiles then pushes his cart away.

the pasty waiter brings me the ticket,
I pull out the plastic,

Kerry Moyer

    wait for the receipt to sign it,
    and we walk out of
    the Eastern Dragon
    until I need some magic again.

Rust & Weeds

Kerry Moyer

[In Rain]

Rain comes when I sit quiet, dry,
in a room, wet lines gently streaming
down windows, or while driving, fat drops fall
on windshields, explode, scatter,
across tempered glass, over
miles, sometimes while walking
outside, light pitter-patter rain taps
on my head, runs down my face,
reminding me that rain always falls
from above, onto wherever
I am below.

Rising

Brown water whips,
whirls, spins, while rising
up rough, mossy bark, drowning
ancient oaks. Muddy waters
move, flow fast, foam
under a stone arch bridge.
Branches, sticks tumble, twist,
heavy gray clouds roll slowly,
across dark, brooding skies
to bring more rain, while people
wait; pray the levee holds.

Kerry Moyer

Flint

You can look out
over the green
rolling
tan flint rock
Only rain, wind
Shaping stone
Moving earth
Slow
And it has been
this
For any soul
who cares to see

Wrecked

Wrecked my bike
in Oklahoma. At Bobby's
race, a mud hole grabbed
my muddy tire, threw
my left shoulder into
hard ground, my shoulder
wrecked, now I've lost
my left cross, my left jab,
my left hook, my strength,
my youth–
left at a muddy hole
23 miles outside
of Stillwater Oklahoma.

Kerry Moyer

Harvest

Harvest saw machines
cut wheat.
Acres of gold
weighed, tested
at the elevator.
Farmers in trucks
lined up for scales
to weigh their grain
and hope that moisture
didn't send kernels
home to dry.

Those Threshing Days

In those threshing days:
17, in small Goessel, Kansas
500 people at wheat
field's edge…
New in town to the quiet,
cruel place, Germanic
for generations…bierocks
and zwiebacks and strudel
and I know I'll never
be offered a true place
at that table.

with Kevin

Kerry Moyer

Mending

The cedar post...
holding rusty barbed wire,
boys walking the line,
mending it with pliers,
tall grass brushing,
over faded blue jeans;
Eastern breeze,
bringing bold summer scents
to blanket the pasture,
mingling with diesel fumes
from harvesters cutting grain
a quarter mile away.

A bumblebee bumbling,
buzzing around
sweat staining hats
while a hawk descends:
snatching a rabbit–
then it is off to eat–
fenced cows feeding
on rich prairie grass
don't seem to notice.

The boys finish a side,
pat each other
on dusty backs;
returning to the house
for cold sweet tea,
hot showers, and needed sleep.
The burnt orange disk
setting in the west
sinks below the horizon

Rust & Weeds

in the darkened distance
and another summer day
is closed
on the Kansas plains.

Kerry Moyer

Trash Truck

Trash truck motor roars,
air brakes whine
from half a block away;
startles me awake
rubbing sleepy eyes
rushing out the door,
scurrying barefoot
down icy, cold steps
to push the trash can
to the curb by the street,
and the driveway is frozen
and the small rocks, and small twigs
hurt bare feet.
I get the can to its place
shivering, waving
to the man in the trash truck
just in time to see him work
while telling myself,
next time I will remember
to put the damn trash out
the blessed night before.

Joy

Joy is hot soup
on a cold day,
soft fur under
a gentle hand,
a child's laugh,
a woman's smile.

Joy is the might
of a strong back,
what one can do
with strong hands,
what one can do
with fertile land.

Joy is beauty,
admiring a body:
curves, lines,
flowing hair,
hips, thighs.
Passion's moans, cries.

Joy is a bird's song,
the sound of trains,
God's wild things,
running naked,
reckless
through towering trees.

Joy is the seasons
and what they bring.
It is the air in my lungs,
the gift of another day
in God's light.

Kerry Moyer

Alone

Sometimes–
I feel alone.
Strong stone box
enclosing me
in cold, hard rock.
So far from God,
in deepest dark.
Sometimes–
I feel alone.

Quiet

He roamed through the thick,
choking quiet of loss.
Creaking boards,
pile of ads, unopened bills
on a dusty desk top.

Sitting down,
dropping his face
into waiting hands.
A long breath moves
through air that holds
the lingering scent of her.

Rising to weary feet,
the man grabs his keys,
walks out his door
into a world
he doesn't know anymore.

Kerry Moyer

Stare

I can sit and stare at nothing,
sit and stare at random people,
sit and stare at cats being cats,
dogs being dogs,
colorful graffiti on trains, buildings.

I can stare in the mirror,
stare into the eyes of strangers,
stare at the naked sky:
the sun, moon, rising, falling.

Stare at the depth of my sin.
Stare at the state I'm in.
Stare at what is in front of me.
Stare in the rearview at what's behind.
I can sit and stare at nothing.

Cocked

I cocked my lips,
shot words out,
thoughts racing,
piercing ears, hearts,
and they hear

Truth...

Soon to be forgotten,
right after I leave the room,
and they return to sipping lukewarm
coffee in their cubicle prisons.

Kerry Moyer

Pulsing

I used to drink
rum, whiskey,
to be brave, bold,
to move through
loud, pulsing rooms,
find a beautiful girl,
dance, say sweet things,
fall into her,
get wrapped in warmth,
blanketed in heat
to feel anything but me.

Rust & Weeds

Kerry Moyer

Faces

Some faces say
everything...
they would speak
with their mouths, those
poison, pristine smiles,
some faces frown,
turn sour for no reason
whatsoever,
that you would know.
Sometimes dour, dank faces
are found squeezed together,
a terse, tangled troupe
of judging, squinted eyes,
turned up nostrils,
jutted chins chiming
for some small thing,
a trivial slight
from some trivial night
on a day you don't remember,
because you know,

Humans

and all their silly, senseless
petty, pointed faces
thrown like daggers
for no reason you would know
or would they be so kind as to share
From where they sit
way over there?
Where those better people
make bitter faces and mingle...

Light

Moonlight, starlight,
my eyes pulled
to a Kansas sky
seen between
cottonwood trees,
branches dressed
in triangular leaves.

Street lamps
shine down
on cracked,
gray asphalt
on quiet streets
as bugs ascend,
drawn up to light.

A cat watches: eyes
lit, fierce, fixed,
crouched in a yard
as I walk, wander.
A movement and
it darts, a black blur
across my path.

Cigarette smoke finds
my nose,
a red ember glows
bright, moves,
dark silhouette sits
on a darkened
front porch.

Kerry Moyer

A siren sound
finds my ears,
flashing red
draws my eyes,
while walking past
darkened houses,
parked cars, trucks.

At a well lit corner,
another glowing lamp
shines down, on the cat
still watching, now by a curb
while swarming bugs
are drawn to light.
My eyes, lured to light.

Marble

Past a black wrought iron gate,
a marble angel weeps,
perched atop a marble stone
for a child that died
twelve years ago.

Walking toward a tree I know
to find the grave of one I love
I always stop and say hello
to the little boy who sleeps.

While his marble angel weeps,
atop his marble stone,
shedding marble tears
that never touch
the ground below.

Kerry Moyer

Vampire

If I bleed drops on the page,
would you lick the words?
If I wrote my thoughts,
would you drink my curse,
take it as your own?
All the verses that flood me,
all the lines that run
thick, red. This crimson
script, like a sharpened
scroll that pierces my heart.
I'm right here on this page,
would you leave anything
for me?

Kerry Moyer

[In Waters]

Sometimes I look for waters.
Waters that move over rock,
through sand. Waters
that move between trees.
Rivers that wind around hills, valleys,
seas that live in stories
or memories. Deep ocean waters
that hold my thoughts.
Shallow waters where I float, alone
eyes closed. Waters, far away.

Kerry Moyer

Sun Kil Moon

Mark plays
haunting chords,
plucked notes
on his guitar,
words roll out:
Dramamine dreams,
Ohio calling me
and I'm moved
through song after song.
Mind floating
among his leaves
and mine.

Master

Former student bows,
shakes my hand in the mall,
says "Master"
and I think:
all that time spent;
punches, strikes, kicks;
hands, knees, elbows, feet;
focus and forms;
blocks, bruises
each gold bar...
measuring time.
Being taught, teaching
for that title
and I smile.

It has been five years
since I strapped that belt
around this growing waist;
we talk for a bit
about this and that
until we go our separate ways,
far from that time
and those martial days.

Kerry Moyer

The Round

We move in circles,
linear thrust with a right jab,
he moves left,
rear leg round kick lands,
contacts right red target
with a thud,
elbow too late to block it.

One point.

Four minutes and fatigue already setting in,
mouthpiece pushed out
from their parched lips,
needing more air,
hands drop and dangle,
sweat dripping from matted hair,
I change my angle,
close on the red center dot,
throw a left reverse punch
that my tired opponent can't stop,
their spin crescent misses high,
judge steps in
as a buzzer ends the round,
sends red to his corner,
tired, defeated.
I see it in his eyes
going to my corner,
drenched, hot,
but confident,
taking my mouthpiece out,
I drink cool, needed water
and wait…

Meat Soup

Walking out over sand
into the Gulf at dusk,
dark, briny, water covers
feet, ankles, calves,
knees, thighs and waist.
Water is warm, thick.
Moving further from the shore,
broth covers my chest,
chin, inches above
the black glass surface

Typical depth for a shark attack,
three to six feet.
Typical time for a shark attack,
dusk.

I recall a conversation
with this blonde shop clerk,
talking shark attacks,
two this year, at dusk, in three
to six feet of warm briny
water. I think "scars are cool
I'd fight the fish, keep the teeth."

Something brushes my leg.
I am meat floating in soup.
My bravado wanes; I wade briskly
back to my friends and several
dead translucent blue jellyfish:
scattered on the beach.

Kerry Moyer

Kalashnikov

Mikhail Kalashnikov
never made a ruble.
7.62×.39 round, Mikhail
Kalashnikov's cheap stamped
metal, gas operated, bullet
delivery system. Soviet
Avtomat Kalashnikova,
1949 and the Warsaw
Pact. That rifle slung over
Vietcong shoulders, Jihadi
shoulders, American militia
shoulders over years, muzzle
velocity of 2250 feet per
second. Supersonic rounds tearing
holes, breaking bones. High
capacity death dealer.
The people's rifle, the worker's
rifle, absolutely reliable, efficient.
Comrade Mikhail's creation
found in Afghan mountains,
wooden cabinets, leaning
against walls, in Baghdad,
Moscow, Minneapolis, ready
to send bullets wherever
that muzzle points.
Mikhail Kalashnikov
never made a ruble.

Clicking

Soul sucked,
pulled in,
app owns you,
sells your thoughts,

sells you.

To a conglomerate
with your neighbor
and their neighbor
and their neighbor,

packaged.

Floating
on a glowing page.
World. Wide. Web.

Forever

and ever
and ever,
we keep clicking
and clicking,
willing slaves
on a digital auction block,
and we know it
and

we.
don't.
stop.
clicking.

Kerry Moyer

Like a Breeze

I remember you

walking to your car,
away to your car,
your back to me, the swing
of your hips,
in that sundress that stopped above your knees,
I remember walking after, following
the bounce of your hair with my
eyes, heart like a brick,
feet like bricks,
thoughts knotted, heavy,
like bricks,
I never saw you again.
You left like a breeze
and every now and then I feel--
you on my neck

like a breeze...

Warm Water

Standing under
falling warm water,
moving over skin.
Soap suds ride,
run down
to the drain
where they
whirl, swirl, spin.
The "Staunton Lick"
plays from my phone,
sitting next to Michelle's soap,
clear from Oklahoma;
smells like peace,
wheat fields, red dirt roads...
I smile in gentle thought,
led by water
warm water sounds,
the slow, steady
beat of my heart.

Kerry Moyer

Brute

The brute in me
broods,
frowns and fumes,
finds a fierce look,
drowns in rage,
fights my heart,
the soft parts
that are wrapped
in kindness,
the parts that stall
my storm,
the parts that love
and remember
who I was:
the shadow that waits,
sits and waits.

Iron

His grip, strong,
hand like an iron tool.
We spoke about the weather,
how Kansas makes a game of it.
Seasons play charades,
and calendars mock the days.
For a short spell we sat,
the Man's granite face cracked,
and a genuine smile formed
where a frown had been
just moments before.

Kerry Moyer

Dust

When I was small
grandmother told
of black blizzards that
choked towns, fields—
jackrabbit, locust plagues
killed farmers' crops.

Grim folks with kerchief-
covered faces coughed,
shuttered windows,
stuffed rags under doors
as brown powdered earth
covered every floor.

And day turned to night,
long-eared jackrabbits
moved in darkness,
covered in dust,
while prairie preachers prayed
to the God of Abraham.

Rust & Weeds

Kerry Moyer

If I Wrote the Last Poem

If I wrote the last poem
I'd ever write:
The sky is on fire
burning away everything.
What words would find their way
onto the doomed, useless page?
Soon to be consumed in flames?
Would I write about the glow
coming over the scorched horizon?
Our hopeless state?
Write about what had been
before armageddon?
Would I lament the end?
Start counting my sins?
Carve notches into my skin?
Give my pound of flesh
for everything I did
against God and man?
Would I find my wife, my children?
Tell them I love them
and to close their eyes?
Wrapping bloody, carved arms around them
while the burning sky fell?
Write about how I can't save them
from the falling conflagration?
Our existential situation:
Piles of ash
on blackened ground...

[In Wind]

Kansas west wind, God's hand
    pressed against
my chest, tall grass
    bends, but I don't, pedal
hard as I can
    over gravel,
over dirt, over
    rock

with Kevin

Kerry Moyer

Cramps

Hip flexors twitch,
pedal stroke cramps
legs, hips, feet.
Traveling cramps,
hellish pain, I almost
vomit. Two riders roll by,
tip their covered heads.
Dusty sunglasses,
dusty bikes, rider asks
if I'm okay, words come
out "I'm fine, thanks"
and I'm so tired. I pop
an electrolyte tab, slam
Roctane, Gu. Sickening sweet
paste, sugar mouth, chapped
lips, left hand, numb, then zingers
shooting pains into toes,
crippling, muscle, twisting
cramps, my thoughts, dark,
so tired, so tired, twisting,
curving roads, I look up
from bars, a mile of rolling
hills ahead, maybe two,
cold rain comes on, my teeth
chatter, I'm off the bike to walk
a hill. Any pedaling and I–
cramp, cramps moving
through muscles and my
legs don't work. A long-haired
older guy offers words,
another rider on a Salsa
slings pickle juice, more
words like whispers,

Rust & Weeds

distant, miles from my
dirty, tired legs
I pedal, I pray,
Road 20 is muddy,
chunky, daunting derailer-
breaking flint rock, limestone
steps, ruts, punchy, short,
spirit-killing climbs, I think,
speak aloud to God, between
heavy breaths, I can't break
my bike–
Around 30 miles
from the Kanza chute
cramps ease, legs work
again, GLORY, they work again.
I clear my head, thank God, think–
don't forget to eat, drink now.
Can't have them come back,
just can't have them come back,
I see a dusty, defeated guy is off
to the side, leaning on a dead,
twisted tree, glassy eyed, bike
lying on the ground, in grass
by a leaning fence. He looks lost,
listless. I tell him, I tell myself.
You're almost there.
The hard part's over,
again, the hard parts over–
He looks at his dusty shoes.
He looks at his dusty bike.
He looks up at wispy clouds,
then brings his eyes to mine.
It's cramps, he says
It's cramps...

Kerry Moyer

Cold, Yellow Towel

At mile 80,
off my bike to sit
on the chaise lounge
while Salsa guy snapped a pic
This route was new, hot, long,
I'm Kahola crushed, drip-dried

My body wanted to quit
heat exhaustion had set in
and cramps for 70 miles
but my friends got me home
We moved kind of slow

Cheers, cow bells
while coming down the chute
I high-fived a couple of guys
cheers, cow bells
Heard my name called
cheers, cow bells

A hug from Jim
Then the damndest thing
This young woman
put a cold, yellow towel
on my hot, sunburned neck
and it was joy
pure.damn.joy.

with Curtis

Stained Red

28 degrees,
chilled human mass,
gravel bikes,
red, golden disc
breaking through
brilliant blue
Oklahoma sunrise.

Cannon blast
starts the test,
pedal strokes roll
wheels over Oklahoma
red earth.

Rattlesnake hills,
steep climbs,
legs scream,
mind bleeds mud,
red roads wind
through my thoughts.

The chute,
Bobby's hug
wrapped around
those red dirty few
who grew.

103 hard miles
stained red
in my memory.

Kerry Moyer

Solitude

Riding north
my path,
rough, rutted
from recent rains;
watching my line,
pedaling past green,
covered ears of corn
swaying gently
to the left of me.
I breathe deep,
needing time to think;
I scroll through the day,
ponder, pray,
meditate, speculate,
send silent wishes
floating up to God
while the sun looks on–
its brilliance
blinding,
warming rays
remind me to drink
on a hot July evening;
the crunch of tires
rolling over rock,
crickets chirp,
south wind whispers,
nature's sermon sings,
my mind slows
while I find solitude
on a Kansas gravel road.

Stubble

The stubble on my neck,
thick, coarse hair,
I take rough hands,
put white shaving cream
there, below my trimmed
gray beard, shown
in the bathroom mirror,
bringing the razor,
chin lifted high,
two thousand years,
chins lifted high,
blades brought to thick
forest whiskers, to stone chins,
reflected in ponds, rivers, lakes,
in polished steel,
on polished blades.
Roman men wore
smooth stone chins,
jaws like river rocks.
Fathers' white whiskers were
thick, full, our name, Germanic.
Visigoths, Ostrogoths. Vandals,
nomadic tribes wore fierce, virile beards.
We fought river rock Romans
in forests, in fields, across rivers, ponds,
lakes, until that Empire fell.
Generations back, miles of stubble,
blades cut barbaric, savage
looks from faces, chins
staring into mirrors, into ponds.
Two thousand years
and here, in this glass I gaze
while the razor glides

Kerry Moyer

    down my neck, steel cutting
    away three days' growth.
    Visigoth, Ostrogoth, Vandal,
    the blade brought to bear,
    this ritual, this passage,
    over twelve thousand days ago.

Kerry Moyer

Weary

The gray is becoming white.
My face framed
in the colors of age,
crows feet forming
at the corners of my eyes,

I'm weary.

The blue less bright
with fading sight,
print t-shirt covers
a diminished chest,
arms divested of brawn,
and damned if I'm not weary.
Middle age pulling the strength
from legs and grinding knees,
blue jeans hide the atrocities,
even my soul feels old sometimes,
but I can't see those lines.
Father Time slipped in,
switched out all that was young
for this mass,
body breaking down,
at war with my spirit,
whispering,

I'm weary.

Feel the faint tick of time,
in my bones,
behind my eyes,
an exhale,
this restless ghost,

Kerry Moyer

waiting to roam,
on my way to dust,
moans,

I'm weary.

Squinting to see it,
reading the small print
on a bottle I bought,
renew the gym membership,
get biceps again,
color my hair,
look into the magic mirror,
lie to myself,
take another pill.
Father Time,
Grand Grifter,
Brutal Timeline Drifter,
answers in the space between the ticks,
the rhythmic tock,
looking back from the mirror,
reflection speaks clearly,

You are weary.

Unsinkable

Harland and Wollf's pride.
The great boat hit a
chunk of ice. Now it lies
still in cold northern waters.
Broken tea cups, bent metal
litter barnacle encrusted floors
walked by ghosts.
The unsinkable White Star ship
rests with Captain Smith,
deep in my thoughts,
when they drift and wander.

Kerry Moyer

Age

Age is a weight that pulls everything down, I'm falling, collapsing like Rome, like carved stone, beaten by rain, wind, time, fractured between heat and cold, brought low, eroded by life's seasons.

Twenty-Five Years and Not a Stone

All the outbuildings gone
from tack shed to chicken coop
I slow
my car, look up
the long dirt drive...
the house gone
where I used to live,
that farmhouse outside
of Goessel Kansas.
Twenty-five years and not
a stone remembers.
A grass blade breeze
like memory...

with Kevin

Kerry Moyer

Missile

In football:
I'd launch myself
like a missile
at a number,
every down,
people watched,
people roared,
as we launched our bodies
like missiles,
like violence,
while parents
cheered, watched
and roared.

Night Moves

Flames dancing in windows,
sirens screaming,
fire trucks flashing,
grease fire spreading–
That red brick building
on Sixth Street–
Water shot
from hoses
while we watched
from across the street–
Those hardwood bar tops
marked, carved, loved,
drinks served
over days, years–
Bruff's burning.

People stood around,
two blonde girls crying;
a guy in glasses said,
It's gotta come back
then again, more like a question,
It's gotta come back?

Kerry Moyer

James Wanted to Fight

James wanted to fight.
After school,
over nothing.
Foul smelling and a crooked grin:
he harassed, haunted the halls,
he would not stop asking, telling;
so a time was set:
4:00 pm on a Friday.

We fought,
surrounded by kids
who watched and cheered,
they wanted blood.
Bored teenagers
congregated in an empty lot
across from Nick's house:
Charlie was the ringmaster,
squared us up.

Almost immediately,
I punched James in the head.
Hard Left jab landed
above his right eye.
A loud thud,
look of shock
on his zit-covered face.
Then he popped me in the lip,
just caught me;
I tasted blood, felt it swell,
but I hit him harder,
a lot harder.
He was staggered, slow.
He moved back, back.

Moving and backing,
not swinging,
hands doing nothing.

He was beat.
He knew it.
I knew it.
Both of us tired,
me from swinging,
him from retreating.

Charlie stepped in,
called it;
next day everyone said
I won.
I was thinking about this
fight from forever back
because I read James had died:
drugs and alcohol.
I'd heard a hard life,
and I wanted to care more
but couldn't.
He was just an asshole
who wanted to fight me
over nothing.

Kerry Moyer

Empty

If I
could empty

myself

of all those things,
those empty things,
I might find myself

less empty.

Rust & Weeds

Kerry Moyer

Brick

While lying in my bed,
putting words onto the page,
Miles came rambling in
and asked If I'd write a poem for him,
a poem about a brick.

He told me the brick was red,
and smaller than a loaf of bread.
I wrote a few lines down,
shared them with my boy,
and asked if he had words to add.

After a while, Miles's eyes
told me it was time for sleep,
and up to his room we went.
He yawned and said,
I love you dad, then flopped
onto his waiting bed.

I kissed him on his head,
gently tucked him in
so he could dream of bricks,
what one can build with them
while sleeping in his wooden bed.

Miles

Miles moves
Miles in his world
Miles from mine
Miles was born
Miles back
Miles traveled since
Miles dug into my heart
Miles deep
Miles smiles
Miles my son

Kerry Moyer

Edward at 13

He's pretzeled in his chair,
a tangle of arms and legs,
my son's blue eyes
locked to a screen.
He looks up and I ask
a question
no one knows, and he's back
to his phone.

I Ate the Last Cookie

I ate the last cookie,
sitting in the pantry
with not a single thought
to who might have wanted
the soft and sweet,
baked piece of heaven.

My children
would enjoy it
as much as I,
but in this moment
I am selfish and greedy:
taking the treat for me
without an ounce of guilt or shame,
until my eight year old
sees the crumbs and asks,
Did you eat the last cookie?

I crack under questioning,
my small child's scrutiny,
and promise to buy him a whole box
when we shop for groceries
the next blessed Sunday.

Kerry Moyer

Moments

When my boys seem broken,
I think to myself:
*I hope they have more of their mother
and less of me.*
In my sad moments, I think:
*the worst of her
is better than the best of me.*

Annette Wore Smiles

Annette wore smiles,

a faded, flowered dress, dingy white socks,
scuffed black shoes,
red bow in dirty, brown hair.

Annette wore smiles,

while boys on the block
mocked, laughed, roared;
girls stared, giggled, whispered.

Annette wore smiles,

skipped, sang songs to the sky,
to the trees, while she shared
her smile with me.

Kerry Moyer

Park Lane

At 15.
Walking through
the Park Lane lot,
two kids I didn't know
walked up on either side–
One on the right asked:
what I'd do if he had a knife,
what I'd do if he took it out,
cut me right there
in the Park Lane lot.
I slowed my pace,
looked right, then left,
thought for a moment
then spoke the only words
I could think to say,

Guess I'd bleed, then we'd fight.

Good answer.
The kid said, smiling
Good answer.
Guy on the other side
was quiet the whole time.

I watched them leave
while finding myself
about fifty feet
from the comic book store
where I was set to spend
the three dollars and change
I had sitting
in my left denim pocket.

Three Rons

The Sunrise apartments,
A place for drunks with no money,
two or three rooms,
booze, dope
were like numbers on the doors.

Ron the Roofer was kind, wore tar in his beard,
had government cheese in a greasy fridge,
smoked weed, drank cheap beer,
his ribs broken by a twelve year old
on a bet dad made that I couldn't hurt his friend.

Ron the painter had painted clothes,
a sad face, a white van that ran,
rows of paint cans on either side
of his door that was never open,
no one ever coming or going.

Ron the Carpenter had a daughter,
her name was Maria and we hung out
on a broken down car by the tracks.
She was pretty and knew things.
I was two years younger, tried to act older.

We watched my dad beat two men
for offering us beer.
Little brother Danny, ran to tell,
dad caught them at the tracks,
hurt them real bad.

After the fight
they walked back by
with bloody faces, said they were sorry
but wouldn't look us in the eye.

Kerry Moyer

Four Kittens

Four kittens:
two yellow, two gray,
abandoned by their mother
in the dead of winter,
found crying and cold,
in loose hay,
on the dirty barn floor.
Father placed them

Gently

in a small wooden box
with a towel from the house.
He placed them by the stove,
warmed them, held them,
fed them tepid milk
from a trembling spoon.
For two days he tried,
but they died on a Sunday

Quiet and Still

in the box by the stove.
Father cried for those tiny lives
lost in the still of night.
I went to bury them in the pasture
while father found things to do
away from me,
and what I set out to do
on that Sunday afternoon.

Rust & Weeds

Kerry Moyer

A Life

My brother works hard,
saves money, fixes things
with some of grandpa's tools;
he drove cool cars,
liked to shoot pool in bars
when he was younger.

My brother is kind,
taught me to tie my shoes
when I was five,
never forgets his nephew's birthdays
or mine.

My brother loves a man
who we claim as ours,
like my sister's husband,
or any other
who came to us through love.

My brother is a survivor,
middle-aged, tested;
he's lost friends to AIDS;
he's lost lots of things;
and he's never hurt a soul.
But, was bullied,
called a "faggot"
in high school.

And, those angry, ignorant souls,
they don't know my brother
or any other man, whose mother
loved and raised them to find
they are just like the rest of us;

Rust & Weeds

they love and live,
hope for peace and the nicer things,
kindness and space
to live how they choose,
free of fear and judgement
openly among the rest of us.

My brother works hard,
saves money, fixes things
with some of grandpa's tools;
he drove cool cars,
liked to shoot pool in bars
when he was younger.

Kerry Moyer

Orange Shirt

Neighbor kid sits in his chair:
high, smoking a cigarette,
loud music blares
from somewhere I can't see;
his dingy orange shirt glows
against the gray painted porch;
his grandmother walks past,
shakes her head at his state,
but he doesn't see,
and I think for a moment
she should hit him
with the rolled up newspaper
that sits a few inches
from her slippered feet,
demand that he mow the grass,
do this or do that,
move from that spot he is planted.
But she won't,
and I will see him there again tomorrow,
always right there again tomorrow.

Morning Dew

Shotsie the mare
was coming due.
It was early spring,
mornings saw a chill
settling over everything.
Shotsie would stand
at the fence not far
from a well traveled road,
running east and west
at the edge of the north pasture.
Father would walk the line
every evening
before night fell
to check on his mare
and what she carried.
Father would talk, over coffee
about how he hoped
the new foal would be
chocolate brown,
wear a white painted face
like the quarter horse
who carried it.

I awoke one morning
to find father shaking,
sobbing on our small
covered porch.
Through halted speech,
eyes clouded with grief,
he spoke slowly
about the foal he found
lying still on new grass,
covered in the sack

Kerry Moyer

>where inside mother
>it had grown.
>In sorrow he recalled
>a chocolate brown coat,
>white painted face,
>not far from a well traveled road.
>
>As spring unfolded
>days warmed, grew longer,
>fields filled with color,
>I'd walk my dog
>past the place
>now flush with green,
>where spring grasses grew
>and new life was lost
>in the cold morning dew.

Rust & Weeds

Kerry Moyer

The Saddle Boogie Saloon

There was a fight every night
at the Saddle Boogie Saloon.
Drunk used car salesmen
in cheap plaid suits
would go to fisticuffs
over a girl, or a crooked look.

Urban cowboys in Stetson hats
would two step,
cut a rug with a lonely woman,
smell of bourbon, English Leather,
hope for a nightcap,
take a cab home later,
flick glowing butts
out cracked windows,
exhale that last drag,
put ten wadded dollars
in the cabbies hand.

On weekend visits,
kids could shoot pool,
quarters all night with dad's
third girlfriend in five weeks,
kids know her
from those "meetings,"
coffee, cigarettes and those
"hi my name is"…greetings,
coffee at twelve years old,
cream and sugar.

Listening to old men
talk about the wagon they fell from
while dancing and fighting,

buying drinks for lonely women
at The Saddle Boogie Saloon.

Kerry Moyer

Clanging

Sometimes the bar
is a lonely place.
Me, with my glass,
people moving around
while I sit
on a stool,
and the clang of glasses,
and chatter,
the muffled
banter,
like clanging in my head.

Sin

I can't look
right at the piles of it:
the mass of my sin.

I can't see it:
all of it piled around me,
pile after pile,
buried in it.

And, I pray
for grace
for God's patience,
and the piles grow.

They grow and grow.

Kerry Moyer

Mercy

Tree tops stick proud
out of blue water.
White caps are pushed
by a north wind toward
the waiting bank, break
on waiting rocks.

Boat drifts, sits basking
under a waking sun.
Snake swims past
a bated line cast toward
waking waters.

Slight tug, glistening line
dips, rod tip bows,
a fish is found.
I rock back, drag giving
inches, hook holding
until the fish tires,
surrendering
to the steady pull
from above.

Last chance, fighting fish
launches, twists, my relentless
reeling, white belly glistens,
gray reflective scales
flash bold, bright
against the ever rising
morning sun.

Bass lands in the boat,
gasps, gills fan out, red,

Rust & Weeds

removing the steel hook
I see the size of my tired,
dying prize.

Mercy takes hold,
and I release my catch
back to the waters
from which it was claimed.

Kerry Moyer

Arm's Length

An arm's-length away,
his thoughts filled that space,
as she slinked, moved soft
in front of his wanting eyes,
and she saw, she always saw,
but he knew the miles,
the distance here
and how they couldn't touch;
how they could never touch.

December

I see you in the dark,
the light. In the space
between day and night.
Sometimes a sound,
finding my ear,
a voice I knew,
a north wind's cold
whisper moving through
each December.

Kerry Moyer

Magnolia

I missed you,
for a moment,
when I stopped to look
out the north window
at my magnolia tree
flowering in spring.

I wondered,
but for a moment,
thoughts floating to you
like a dream from my youth
like white blossoms falling
to the speckled ground.

Rust & Weeds

Kerry Moyer

Lilacs

Heady, sweet, fleeting–
the scent of lilacs,
my thoughts,
a garden.
Those lives
found resting
in my soil,
long after they have gone
and that is the gift:
the scent of lilacs,
heady, sweet, fleeting,
never far from me,
or where my thoughts
plant those seeds.

To Nap

Today–
I move from here to there,
mind strapped
with thought, caught in noxious
noise, the numbing daze
of everyday gazing up
at the sky, I think and fly
over pulsing power lines–
I follow the wind's
wild, wandering path.
Crash through clouds,
hues of blue, white,
black speckled night
until that current slams bold
against whatever broke
that fearless, turbulent stroll.
Falling to the ground–
I am exhausted from the ride,
looking around I find green
grass, ancient trees, soft, serene
expanse, a sleepy, quiet
land to take a needed nap
while the world screams
miles and miles from me
and where I fell to dream.

Eyes

Eyes like mirrors,
like poison spears,
like matchsticks burning,
searching at periscope depth.
Eyes like snares, traps,
like the eyes of an asp.
Eyes that find me,
blind me to everything
outside of their all consuming
view and all that they see.

Rust & Weeds

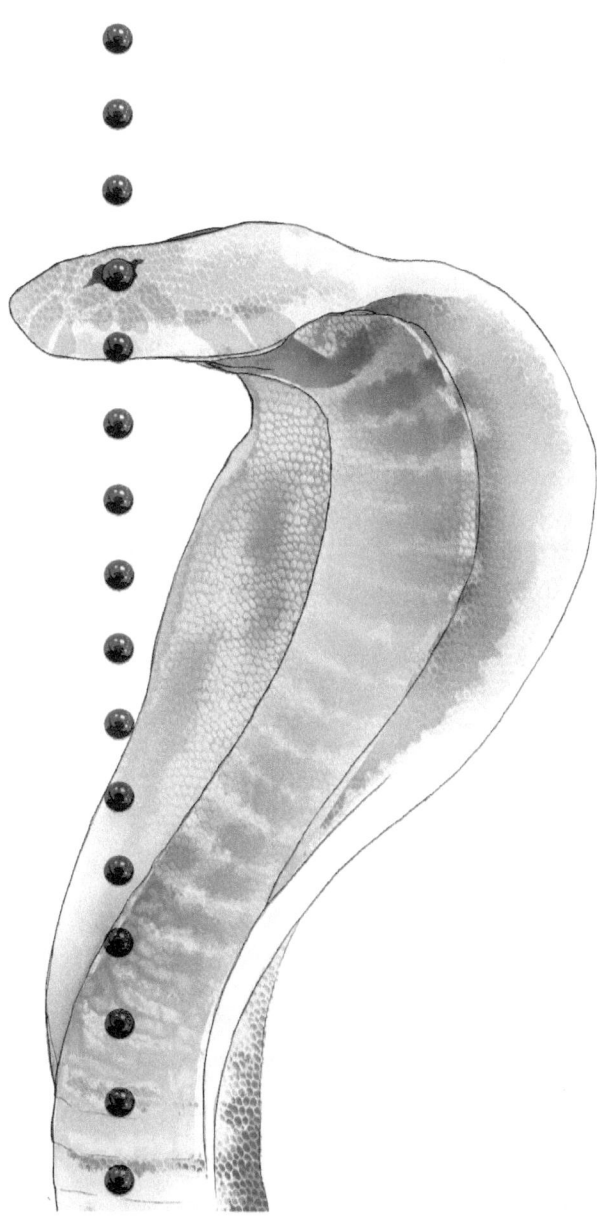

Kerry Moyer

I Wake

I Wake–
Mind moves in sand,
last thought: a dream,
a scene hung on the edge
of clouded memory.
Out my window,
pear tree holds the moon,
white circle sits,
seems to bounce
on a branch bearing fruit,
wrapped in night,
cat moves over my sheet,
pressure on my feet
from feline weight,
a yawn escapes,
the dream held promise,
I think.
This feeling says *yes*
as it teeters
on the edge of waiting sleep,
on the edge of waiting dreams.

Fog

If I found a path
through the haze–
would it carry me
to a clear place?
Far from the spaces
I feel lost?

If I took each breath,
filled my chest, with precious air–
Would I inhale happiness?
Exhale everything less?

If I could shout
across the world
Stop all of this!
For the love of God,
for the love of Peace,
sit still and listen
to each other
if only for one solid minute!
Would any soul lend an ear?

If I could find rest,
share that secret
with all who care to hear it,
just lie down,
be still,
cover yourself in quiet,
be filled,
feel
the beat of your heart,
try not to lose yourself
in life's ashen fog.

Kerry Moyer

Damage

If you would have been
loved, life would have felt
better when you were young,
before your broken fell onto me.
You may have smiled more, found
joy in your reaching boys. If
you would have been
loved, we would not spend
so much time building
what could have been,
what should have been.

Worth

A life
where work
makes up your worth
more than all those things
you do, away from there,
I'd say is sad.

If you work every minute
of every day,
a head empty
of anything to say,
or share,
as lifeless as
the product you place
on a store shelf.

A life
with no music,
void of taste,
no sweet things,
I'd say is tragic.

So many marching shells,
wandering the streets,
living lives without living,
anywhere you care to see.

Kerry Moyer

Sometimes

Sometimes

You are a stop
on the road,
a snapshot
tucked away in a drawer,
an album
in an attic box,
sitting by the attic door.

Sometimes

You are a phone booth
at the edge of the world,
taking a quarter
for some thoughts,
a time and place,
left like litter on the floor.

Sometimes

We are fading ink,
found fleeting,
passed with the turn of a page,
in the blink of a wandering eye,
lost to fading, passing time.

But, sometimes we are more.

Sometimes we are more.

Ghost

I just want to rest.
It says again and again
in my listening ear,
keeping me
from needed sleep.

Dark shadows move
just beyond my lantern's light.
Dark shadows move
in me
where no light can reach.

How long has he walked
these narrow halls?
How long has he wailed,
trapped between
these cracked, plaster walls?

I can not help
the shade that haunts
this small apartment space;
I just want to rest–
and, I'm too tired to be afraid…

Kerry Moyer

Sharp Teeth

Sharp teeth tear, silver tongues
preach, pontificate, prey
on people. Slithering grifters grab
all the gold. Gilded beasts
ply people with blinding lies
and those marvelous
monster eat the world.

Dusk

To the west
a blazing sphere
sits behind hanging,
gray clouds.
My eyes tethered,
watch the slow
descent behind
black distant trees,
crouched beyond fields
of fervent green.
Caught in memory,
a thousand dusks
whisper *God,*
and I stand
small–
covered in golden
rays of closing day,
finding peace
in what the setting sun
had to say.

Kerry Moyer

Sunshine

When the thoughts are so heavy
I think, I just think,
no rope could possibly pull
me from those ragged teeth,
the wounds they bring.
If I could just find the light,
feel sunlight on my face,
warm sunshine on my face,
rays to push out my night.

Rust & Weeds

Kerry Moyer

The Patience of Saints

My wife smiles,
drinks coffee, bakes, dabbles
in the patience of saints,
buoys me to hope,
ties me, binds me to now,
rolls in the waves
of my tempest,
holds my hand,
shows me how
to live.

She pulls me from the shifting,
sinking sand of a mad,
melancholy, ever moving mind,
brings quiet, beautiful calm,
a smile that soothes, reassures,
levies the wave-battered banks
of a wounded, unsure soul.
My wife braves the bitter, finds my light,
sometimes with little thanks,
sometimes in the dark of night.

We love–
an imperfect, perfect love,
found by chance,
or a gift from God above.
My wife smiles,
drinks coffee, bakes,
dabbles in the patience of saints,
buoys me to hope,
gives me a smile I wear
in the solitude of us.

About the Author

Kerry Moyer resides in Emporia Kansas with his wife Sarah and their boys Edward and Miles. Kerry is the author of two Chapbooks "Let's Start with That" and "these boys" along with his first poetry collection *Dirt Road* and this volume of poetry. He is an active member of Kansas Author's Club and the Emporia Writer's Group. Kerry has worked in community mental health working with youth and young adults for twenty years. His interests outside of writing include cycling where he has participated in gravel cycling events like the Dirty Kanza which calls Emporia and the Flint Hills home. Kerry also holds a fifth-degree black belt in Taekwondo and first-degree black belt in Hapkido. "Master Moyer" taught martial arts and self-defense for over a decade and continues to be sporadically involved in the martial arts world. Kerry enjoys creating arts and crafts as well as playing music on his guitar when he can. Kerry is inspired as a writer by the people, communities, and landscapes of Kansas and the Midwest.

A Note of Thanks

I want to thank my wife **Sarah** and our boys **Edward** and **Miles** for continuing to inspire and support me as a husband, father, and poet. They are my strength. Much thanks going out to all my friends and family who have supported me as a writer and as a human.

I would like to name a couple of individuals for their specific contributions to the book and their part in all of this. To **Curtis Becker**, I need to give special thanks. As my editor, publisher, and constant source of support, thank you from the bottom of my heart. Thank you for your friendship! I got to give a big shout out to **Kevin Rabas** for being my Yoda, my teacher, and most importantly, my dear friend. To coffee, side-kicks in Starbucks and other interesting moments, I have enjoyed our adventures over coffee. You've made me a better poet. I look forward to future writing time together and caffeine fueled adventures. **Curtis** and **Kevin**, thank you both for collaborating on a few of pieces in the book. That was fun.

I would like to give a special thank you to **Allysa Hallett**. for creating the cover and illustrations. They help bring my words to life.

To my friends in the **Emporia Writers Group** and **Kansas Authors Club**, thank you all for the support you've given through your words and actions. It is a thrill to be involved with so many talented, creative and supportive people.

Thanks to **Gravel City Roasters** and **Joe**, among others, for keeping me caffeinated during hours of edits with **Curtis**! Actually, I'd like to thank coffee. Much love to coffee.

Thank you to **Marcia Lawrence** and **Ellen Plumb's City Bookstore** for all you've done for writers and this community.

Huge thanks to the **Kansas** I love, it's people, blue skies, sunrises, sunsets, and all those roads I've traveled.

Thanks and love going out to the **gravel tribe** for those friendships and countless two wheeled adventures.

Last but certainly not least, thanks to **God** above for each day of living, surrounded by friends and family and all the gifts this life has afforded me.

Praise for Rust & Weeds

Not only "Rust and Weeds" but the sharp blade and uncommon blossom of ordered, plain-spoken verse; Moyer's poems grow more glorious in tone and color in this new (his fourth) collection. He is a warrior. In this collection his aesthetic muscle begins to show.
 -**Kevin Rabas**, Poet Laureate of Kansas, 2017-2019, *On Drums*

Kerry Moyer is at his best when writing about the everyday subjects that are part of his soul. Through his poems, you can experience long rides on gravel roads deep in the Flint Hills, the sting surrounding loss of people and places, and the deep love and loyalty he has for his family. Moyer's poetry is rooted in a landscape familiar to many rural Kansans, and it is easy to see through his well-placed images how this landscape has touched him throughout his life. In Rust and Weeds, Kerry Moyer firmly establishes himself as a "dirt road" poet, a poet for all of us who call the dirt roads and prairies of Kansas home.
 -**Lindsey Bartlett**, *Vacant Childhood*

Kerry Moyer is a poet with a young heart and an old soul who celebrates his beloved Kansas and the people who make it special. The poems in Rust & Weeds are glimpses of life in the Midwest, often bright with color, sometimes shrouded in gray. Moyer writes, "So very little impresses me anymore," followed a few pages later by an ode to the small things that bring him joy. Moyer's eye and ear for detail capture the contradictions that make our lives unique and so much like one another.
 -**Mike Graves**, *Shadow of Death*

Kerry Moyer is a rare find–brilliant in introspection and empathy. Moyer's poetry is savory and satisfying. This is a poet who examines pathways, searches, and finds, layered meaning in all aspects of life's experiences, a poet who never stops thinking, a poet who gifts readers with nature's beauty. Moyer's verse yields simplicity and profoundly inspiring observations.
 -**Ronda Miller**, *I Love the Child*

www.ingramcontent.com/pod-product-compliance
Lightning Source LLC
Chambersburg PA
CBHW021411290426
44108CB00010B/475